HAYWIRE

May Swenson
Poetry Award Series

HAYWIRE

poems
by

George Bilgere

UTAH STATE UNIVERSITY PRESS
Logan, Utah

Utah State University Press
Logan, UT 84322-7800

Cover art by David Wilder
Cover design by Barbara Yale-Read
Manufactured in the United States of America

Library of Congress Cataloging-in-Publication Data

Bilgere, George, 1951-
Haywire : poems / by George Bilgere.
    p. cm. -- (May Swenson Poetry Award series)

    ISBN-13: 978-0-87421-646-2 (cloth : alk. paper)
    ISBN-10: 0-87421-646-X (cloth : alk. paper)
    ISBN-13: 978-0-87421-647-9 (pbk. : alk. paper)
    ISBN-10: 0-87421-647-8 (pbk. : alk. paper)

    I. Title. II. Series.
    PS3552.I425H39 2006
    811'.54--dc22

                                                2006012212

For Jodie

CONTENTS

ACKNOWLEDGMENTS

My thanks to the journals in which the poems below appeared or are forthcoming:

Chattahoochee Review: Aria, Retards

Comstock Review: View of the City of Delft

Denver Quarterly: Haywire

Fulcrum: Closing Time (reprinted here as Happy Hour), Museum Piece, Simile Practice

The Georgia Review: That's a Take

The Iowa Review: Good Humor

The Journal: She's Good

Meridian: Casablanca

The Mid-America Poetry Review: Once Again I Fail to Read an Important Novel, Tosca

Missouri Review: Waiting

Poetry: Janitorial, The Surgeon General

Rattle: Unwise Purchases

River Styx: Miss December

Tar River Poetry: Citizen Kane, Norelco, The Table

I understood the danger of judging this competition right away—I'd be looking for poetry I myself would like to have written. And for the political subject matter that obsesses me in this age of ruthless empire building. No such luck in the manuscripts submitted to me. Not one real rant against the forces attacking our democracy, from the inside or the outside. No book of poems from the Iraqi front—that would certainly have been a strong contender.

So I tried to imagine what May Swenson, the namesake of this book award, would have chosen. She was always one of my guides, with her instinct for the precise words for what she was talking about, and best of all an accurate account of events and experience, full of sly imagery that slipped in and out of the closet. From her I learned that poetry is the saying of it. No room for any dogma there, political or religious. She pulls me back into the realm of Poetry, even if we're now in a post-Eliot, post-Marianne Moore, even post-Ginsberg and post-Ashbery age, where anything smacking of High Art is out the window.

One thing I knew from the beginning—I wasn't interested in what I call the torturers of the language, who write without any relation to what and how we really speak, who think that it's poetry because it's unusual. Poetry for me is not inventing fancy ways of saying things, unless it's playful. It's *what* it says as much as how—the trick is to find the exact words. And nature description, no matter how clever—landscapes without humans front and center in them—has never interested me. Harder to pass over were the poets whose poetry was part of their struggle for sanity, or poets climbing out of some abyss of failed relationships, or poets who submitted the selected poems of a lifetime, a lifetime dedicated to the Sacred Art. I could see that winning would have meant so much to them. And yet, and yet. . . . And here I must lament the lack of humor in the pile of submissions. Bawdiness would have been very welcome in the litany of sorrows. What dismayed me the most about the entrants, though, is how the world of the poetry workshop, with its fear of emotion masked under the prohibition against something called sentimentality, hovered like a fog.

I knew nothing about the author of *Haywire* when I finally picked up the manuscript—the submissions were anonymous—but even though some of the others were just as proficient, I felt comfortable with this one, even ready to argue with the author, for the poetry raised issues for me. I could tell the poet was a guy. (Actually, for May's sake, I would like to have awarded the prize to a woman poet, and I feel slightly guilty for not doing so. But just as guilty for not giving it to a fellow gay poet.) Not openly political, this poet—you knew from his very first lines—didn't fall for anything phony, the hypocritical discourse the media swamp us with, and his own language is irresistibly no-bullshit, down to earth, even sassy. He's unpretentious, speaks as openly from his feelings as guys in this culture can, and has opera in his life—I dig that, with its sexy overtones. In fact, many of the poems are like operatic arias, bel canto style, with its seemingly easy, soaring melodies. And there is plenty going on in this book. Here, I felt, was an irresistible, not-so-easy, engaging humanness, whereas the brilliant technicians—and there were a number of those in the pile—left me cold. This one is simply a damn good poet. So good, that when I found out who he was, and that he'd already gotten several major awards, one chosen by Poet Laureate Billy Collins, I was dismayed that I hadn't been the one to discover him!

I was even more impressed when I read the title poem "Haywire." It speaks of the staggering changes one lifetime has gone through, relegating the old loon—I identified there!—if not to the tower, then into a back bedroom, a burden, irrelevant. I am still stuck in a time when the youth would be marching not dusty country roads but the streets of towns and cities against the Vietnam war—though, sadly, until there's a draft, that's unlikely to happen again. With the changes that have confronted me in my life, from the Great Depression and bombing the Nazis in WWII, to the persecution of dissent (even original thought) in the Cold War, to the immensities of gay liberation, the electronic revolution and the frightening attacks on our secular traditions today, it's taken all my energy and resourcefulness not to be relegated to the back room myself! It takes fancy footwork indeed, and at my great age I'm not up to jitterbugging anymore. (Or what's the dance step you guys are doing now?)

While so many poets are torturing the language, accepting the role assigned to poetry as an academic discipline, or even a monastic one, George Bilgere sticks to a poetry of inclusion. Which means that if almost anyone would read his poetry, it seems to say, they'd understand it; it's about them too, even if, as another colloquial poet, Gerald Locklin, says with a tolerant shrug, "the people I write for don't read poetry." So Bilgere is not alone in this, and I mention Locklin purposely as an outstanding figure among a lot of southern California poets, who like many poets around the country (in a world which proclaims the subject of poetry is language) are also insisting on a poetry that uses language that's almost unobtrusive in order to focus on what it's saying. And speaks *to* someone, is not a solipsistic exercise. It's satisfying that Billy Collins, one of the leading poets of this subtly subversive "school," if one can call it that, was chosen Poet Laureate.

I don't sense any false notes in this book. It is very hard to sound natural like this when the weight of the poetic tradition is in your head, hard not to imitate but to discover what is natural for your own time and place. The poems give a sense of the genuine, of the authentic, not because of the simple language, which is after all the language of the feelings, but because it is grounded in real life. I should stress that if Bilgere is not an overtly political poet, his poem where Christ sits in the electric chair instead of being nailed to the cross, is one of the best poems I've seen against the death penalty. This is a great achievement in a world where we are drenched daily in false simplicities presented as patriotism, from the president on down. Poets have long fled banality, and every poet is faced with the challenge of finding a language to speak his or her own truth. So the most obvious solution, as proposed by Modern Poetry, has been to invent a new language, as many poets have done brilliantly, with elaborations of syntax, innovative word juxtapositions, rich sound. That is a noble endeavor, even if it's not the language very many people understand. But this poet does something harder. He reclaims the language *as it is spoken.* This is American speech transmuted into poetry. And the struggle to do this must be repeated in every generation, to recapture poetry from the forces that want to neuter it.

While I, who can claim to be one of the inspirations for this kind of poetry, go abroad frequently and find great nourishment in foreign cultures and languages, especially when America is launching its imperial mission with optional foreign wars, Bilgere turns his back on that and affirms an almost stay-at-home sensibility. He's been there, he seems to say, and knows the score. If I'm proudly cosmopolitan, his is the true American spirit—not flag waving, but skeptical. Coming from one of the ethnic, industrial cities, there's a gritty element in his work. He recalls all the sorrows of a life—the drunken father, the parents' divorce, his mother's death, his unremitting horniness, his own divorce—nothing special, just what we all have to deal with one way or another. And yet he ends on an almost contented note. *Haywire* is remarkable for being an essentially happy book, though with an ironic eye cast on such happiness while, as he knows, children are starving. And when he arrives at this, we don't say he's avoiding anything, we're glad for him.

Why am I so comfortable with this poet, especially since I keep wanting to argue for more political activism in the poetry? That's just it: I'd be able to argue with him, disagree and still feel we were friends. And I can grant that he may be more centered than I am in this country's spirit. His charm wins me over, and okay, those starving children will be there too, but I'll sit on a bar stool with him anytime.

Edward Field

HAYWIRE

We would give anything for what we have.
                                    —Tony Hoagland

"Give me my leg," she said.
                                    —Flannery O'Connor

I

ARIA

Jussi Bjoerling, that soaring tenor,
  Was pulled down from the air.
My father pulled off to the shoulder

  And closed his eyes. *Nessun Dorma,*
It might have been,
                    or *Cielo e Mar.*

Hotter than Hades in the car
  But I knew enough by then
To shut up. Even my sisters
  For once stopped their idiot fidgeting.

Somewhere that summer, Bjoerling
  Was dying of booze.
My father had lost a lung. No more
  Singing forever.

                    Through the bridal veil
Of a cigarette, my mother
  Stared hard down the highway,
Waiting for it to be over.

BIRDS

You keep reading about them
Vanishing. Or not vanishing,
Exactly, but finding themselves unwelcome.

This morning, for instance,
I stood at the window with my coffee,
Staring across the fields at the new development,
And suddenly heard their silence
From where the trees used to be.
The ruined choirs.

Not one black quarter note
On the drooping measures of the wires.

It was the sound of the new order, half
Breeze in the power lines,
Half ruckus of the highway, that garbage
Disposal of our hunger.

And then,
To make matters worse, a dead bird
Was waiting for me on the sidewalk
As I walked to the CVS
For some more Theraflu.

It always amazes me, the way
Birds seem to have practiced for this
All their lives. Eyes pursed in concentration.
Body cupped in a prayer of wings.

The tiny grip of their claws
On death's invisible branch.

THIS SUMMER

The big-dick rides have taken over
       the Coke-soaked acres
              of Great America.

Now your death-defying, one-hour wait
       is for Big Dude, or the Tower of Power, or even
              the Magnum XL 2000.

              Gone
      are the hokey thrills of yesteryear,

The furtive, darkly vaginal ones, like
       the Haunted House,
                 which was really
the Tunnel of Love,
                 which was actually
the Haunted House.

      They were too slow.
      They took forever.

THE BEAR

The first thing I saw
when I came to visit my friend
in the hospice at the edge of town
was an old woman holding a bear.

She was in a wheelchair on the lawn,
staring out at the lake.
A heavy-set young Candy Striper
was trying to administer some meds
but the woman was nursing her bear
and she wasn't about to stop.

That's how life is.
You enter into it from the darkness
of your mother's womb
and someone hands you a bear.

You hold on for dear life
through nightmares
and a handful of peaceful years.

Then comes a long period of cars and houses,
gardening in the back yard
of that nice bungalow in Des Moines
you and Jim lived in
after he got transferred, sex
passing over you like a fever,
gin and bridge on the porch
in the summer evenings, a war,

and suddenly someone you barely remember
giving birth to one winter
in Chicago, when all the pipes burst,
or was it St. Louis,
is driving you here on a spring afternoon,
the birds singing, everybody
apologizing, finally leaving you

in a wheelchair out on the lawn,
with nothing to do all day but love
your little brown bear, who waited
all this time for you to come home.

THE SURGEON GENERAL

The year he came out with his warning,
like Luther nailing up his theses,
my mother was frying us some salmon cakes
for dinner, or maybe a little Spam,
trying to stretch that dollar
with hominy like white teeth from a can.

Divorce felt like another country.
Suddenly Cassius Clay knocked out
Sonny Liston on our kitchen floor.
My sisters struggled with a Barbie.
Through trees in the back yard
Vietnam moved like bad weather.

In the bathroom a wrinkled girl
with a staple in her navel
presided over my pale,
original boners. 1964.

Somewhere back in St. Louis
lay my pale, original father.
Let the niggers kill each other,
said my mother unto the frying pan,
lighting up yet another
of the million Parliaments
it took to kill her.

THAT'S A TAKE

She's just finished mourning for us all
the fact that spring is here
above the buzz and clatter of this crowded café

where I have stopped reading the paper
because it's impolite to do anything
while Ella Fitzgerald is singing.

And in the pause that follows, I imagine her
turning away from the bright, entranced
face of the microphone,
kidding with the sound technicians

while putting on her hat and a pale green sweater
before she steps out of the studio
and into a spring day as it played out
in 1951, the year I was born,

stopping on the way home at a little deli
to pick up something for supper,
turning words like *macaroni*
and *potato salad*
into tiny American songs
for the pimply kid behind the counter

who thinks nothing of it,
who has his own problems,
who bears his own secret beauty through the world.

SIMILE PRACTICE

When I taught English as a Second Language
the whole class sat down every night
in the Adult Education Classroom
and talked about the strange creature,
the big, unruly language I offered them.

English sound like plastic click together!
said the Vietnamese girl in a voice
like bits of breaking plastic.

Like lot of cricket everywhere,
said the weird kid from Korea,
permanently wired to his Walkman.

Sound like hit a dog with wood stick,
suggested the businessman from Oman,
who resembled a penguin
in the three-piece suit he wore
even in the St. Louis summer.

Yuriko, who just wanted to please,
said, *I'm enjoy English, singing like nightingale,*

while our ill-tempered Italian, Mauricio,
said simply, *Sound like shit.*

And so it went, that wild animal
looming around them, clicking like plastic,
howling like a dog, singing like nightingale,
sounding like shit, until one day

it lifted its heavy, hairy bulk
and shuffled out of the classroom,

leaving the door wide open. And there,
on the varied and ample plain, stood America,
with its malls and soaring cities, its blue jeans
and fast cars full of French fries and breast implants.

And all my students were gone,
for the strange beast they'd studied for so long
had eaten them, each and every one.

ONCE AGAIN I FAIL TO READ AN IMPORTANT NOVEL

Instead, we sit together beside the fountain,
the important novel and I.

We are having coffee together
in that quiet first hour of the morning,
respecting each other's silences
in the shadow of an important old building
in this small but significant European city.

All the characters can relax.
I'm giving them the day off.
For once they can forget about their problems—
desire, betrayal, the fatal denouement—
and just sit peacefully beside me.

In the afternoon,
at lunch near the cathedral,
and in the evening, after my lonely,
historical walk along the promenade,

the men and women, the children
and even the dogs
in the important, complicated novel
have nothing to fear from me.

We will sit quietly at the table
with a glass of cool red wine
and listen to the pigeons
questioning each other in the ancient corridors.

HAPPY HOUR

God created the world
and then vanished into heaven,
Slamming the door behind him.

My father created the world,
then went downtown
to the old Coronado Hotel
with a bottle of Jim Beam.

God still gets angry from time to time,
shaking things up, knocking things down,
drowning and burning anyone who gets in his way.
Then he'll just disappear for a month or two.

My father would show up in the middle of the night,
smash everything in the kitchen, curse creation,
then head out on a three-day bender.

Drop by any church nowadays
and there's not a trace of God inside.
Just an old man looking haunted.

That's how St. Louis feels when I go back to visit.
Big empty streets Daddy used to drive.
The cauldron of our old house, a new family
bubbling up inside.

I can see my father and God
in the now defunct Tack Room at the Chase.
God hated my father. My father hated God.

Shit-faced, they sit there
smiling at each other. Running a tab.

THE MASTODON AT THE CARNEGIE NATURAL HISTORY MUSEUM

You ate lots of vegetation. You were very large.
I love to think of you making love,
perhaps because I'm drawn to big women.

I imagine the dark planets of your eyeballs
rolling in ecstacy above the Monongehela
as a cock thick as my thigh
delivered the news.

Carnegie himself brought you here
a hundred years ago.
He loved doing things like that: *I'm rich,*
I've brought you a mastodon!

You'd see some major changes
if you ever made it out of here.

A black kid in a Steelers jersey
clicks his camera-phone at you
and speaks to the cusp
of glowing plastic: *Mastodon.*

Mass. Toe. Don.

JANITORIAL

All morning he drifts the spacious lawns
like a gleaner, picking up this and that,
the summer clouds immense and building
toward the afternoon, when the heat drives him
under the shade of the oak trees in the quad
and then along cool corridors inside
to pull down last term's flyers

for the chamber recital, the poetry reading,
the lecture on the ethics of cloning,
the dinner with some ambassador,
the debate between Kant and Heidegger,
the frat party, the sorority party, the kegger,
the weekend Bergman festival, the Wednesday
screening of *Dumb and Dumber*. He says
hello to fine young ladies, and tries
not to dwell on their halter tops,
their tanned thighs, shorts up to here.

At five he climbs into an old, dumpster-colored
Olds, lights up and heads home
across the barge-ridden river in its servitude
to East St. Louis, where you know
this poem—glib, well-meaning, trivial—
grows tongue-tied, and cannot follow.

SAY MY NAME

Beyonce's singing,
and what's strange about that
is, first of all, I somehow know who Beyonce is,

and second, the voice I'm hearing
is coming from the earbuds of an iPod
plugged into a kid sitting about thirty feet from me

on the fourth floor of the library
on a humid summer night,
the buzz of cicadas outside

sounding weirdly like the buzz
coming from his head—and third,
I know exactly what he's reading, because

I assigned it to him. It's the immortal
Paradise Lost, by John Milton,
and it's very long and very hard

and it's a terrible thing to be reading
late in the summer, time running short,
life running out, the moon

throbbing just above the trees
and somewhere out there a woman
is leaning against the fender of a car,

waiting for you to shift her
transmission into submission, and God knows
I don't blame this kid for blowing out his ears

at an early age, as Adam and Eve
stand there stunned in the garden,
stupidly covering their crotches, as if

that would do any good, as if it would stop
Beyonce, dark serpent, from reminding
this nice Catholic boy in his brand new

Tommy Hilfiger muscle shirt,
with his fresh, 'round-the-biceps badass
barbed wire tattoo, that in this
fallen world he's never,
never, *evah* gonna get his
smooth white hands on what they burn for.

PETROGLYPHS

Somehow it pleases me to observe,
in the perfect silence of the desert sunset,
that he wasn't very good.
There's really no sense of perspective,
and the men and the deer
he carved on this chunk of sandstone
look pretty much as I would have drawn them
back in third grade.

I suspect that as he labored here
at his stone canvas long ago
he felt the same disappointment
I used to experience as I sat
facing the blank paper
with my new set of watercolors,
so bright and optimistic in their box.

Everything seemed possible,
every doorway to the future
was wide open, until
I made that first botched attempt,
that first failed stroke.

He probably went back
to his little stone encampment
and did something paleolithic
like repairing a spearpoint,
or helping his wife make dinner.

He told her about his day,
standing there in the hot sun
with his sharp stone, trying to make
an image of last summer's deer hunt.

How the creatures looked ridiculous
with their antlers like turkey wings,
and the brave hunters with their spears
ended up looking more like groundhogs
beating the air with twigs.

And that got the kids giggling,
and pretty soon even his wife
found herself unable to be angry with him
for not bringing anything home to eat.
Telling stories was something
he'd always been good at.
and that night as they lay together
before the invention of the roof,
and still a little bit before
the invention of art,
he told her about the deer
and the bison, and the great starry hunter
wheeling namelessly overhead.

Then she rolled over
and showed him a thing or two.

TOSCA

My sister held on to our old turntable
   and all the old records we listened to
through the long Italian opera

of our childhood. So tonight
   we sit in the living room with some wine
and Puccini, as the needle scratches

the black door of the past, the air comes to life
   with that lovely, cornball melodrama,
and our father is sitting in his chair,

ice cubes clinking in his scotch,
   and our mother is in the kitchen
trying to be quiet, trying not to disturb

Maria Callas as she explains
   to Tito Gobbi that she has lived for art
and she has lived for love, but it's hard

to fry pork chops and dice an onion
   without making a certain amount of noise,
and pretty soon my father is shouting at her,

he's trying to listen to the goddamn music
   for Christ's sake, could she for once
show some goddamn respect,

and our mother says nothing,
   it's just the same old argument
between ghosts, after all—the music

won't let them sleep—although
   it has my sister in tears
and even Tosca has begun to weep.

II

VIKINGS

There are always Vikings out there,
  a longboat on the scary edge
     of nowhere.
               Always
a space capsule in the dark,
       Scott and Byrd in their frozen tents,
  Hilary with his Sherpa,
cold men taking measurements.

All of them heroic
    and very lonesome. All of them
far from home.

             Because

  it's here.

Where the rest of us
    are making iced tea.
         Watching *The Jeffersons*
before fixing the screen door.

Now and then
  one of us refuses
to read the newest Harry Potter
  or stand all night in line
for Star Wars.
         Or wear even one
of this summer's disease-
         of-the-month rubberbands,

  quietly choosing our own road
less traveled, our own tent on the tundra.

Expecting no praise for this.
  Receiving none.

MISS DECEMBER

I come upon her
in an old box in the garage
where she's waited all these years,
still lying on her bearskin rug
in front of the cheery fireplace,
still wearing nothing
but her Santa hat
and a friendly smile.

She must be in her sixties now,
somebody's grandmother.
She wears sneakers
and a warm-up suit
to the grocery store.
Her knees are giving her trouble.
Nobody bothers
to airbrush her nipples anymore.

But I remember
the times we had back then
when we were young and crazy,
locked in the bathroom for hours
while my sister pounded on the door.

What the hell, I think,
and take her inside.
One more time,
for auld lang syne.

BLOOD-SOAKED BEAR TURD

> *. . . that sticky infusion, that rank flavor of blood, that poetry*
> *by which I lived . . .*

Close up, the cicada dying on the lawn
was indescribably weird—
a gargoyle fallen from the choir of summer—

but at last I could put a face
to the name he'd been singing
all season long.

Like that time
in a crowded elevator
at some long-forgotten MLA
when my eyes fell on a name tag
reading *Galway Kinnell,*

then rose slowly to a face
terribly altered from the young,
dark-haired dreamer's
in my ancient college anthology
of American poetry,

but indisputably belonging
to the author of *The Bear,*
with its line about the hunter
eating the wounded polar bear's
blood-soaked turd

just to keep himself alive
long enough to eat the bear,

a poem about paying the price
for doing what you're born to do,
singing your one poem all summer,

burning your own body
to make a song of fire.

I smiled at him. He smiled back.
Then the doors opened, and Galway Kinnell
walked down the cold December sidewalk
like anyone else.

RETARDS

Down the street from my sister's house
where I am staying for the summer
of my divorce, is a school
for what we used to call
the mentally retarded.
I sit in the house, trying to work,
listening to their strange cries
from the playground,
their wild articulations.
A little girl is trying to call a boy: *Keith,*
I guess his name is, though it sounds
like *Death,* or like nothing at all,
just a crazy wound on the surface
of the normal, a foghorn meaning
something's wrong out there.

And I think of the look on the faces
of the mothers of retarded kids,
that same tired look of mandatory sainthood
my wife was just learning to master,
and finally, to drown them out,
I put on Brahms, a jittery violin
blending with the cries of the broken children.

Years ago when I lived in Denver
with a woman who defined
one green season in my life, our neighbors
down the street were a retarded couple.
Their yard was perfect, a putting green
of ceramic rabbits and chipmunks
where plaster figures of Snow White
and the Seven Dwarves smiled at the street.

The man and his wife did not work.
In the evening they walked around the block,
hand in hand, smiling but never speaking,
and at twilight we could see them
through the open front door,

sitting before the tv like the rest of us,
as if to say, *See? What you folks do
is not so hard,* and soon
we all began to feel anxious
when we'd mow the lawn or water
the petunias, the retarded couple
mirroring our every move

with a smile, looking past us
through their thick glasses,
going in when we went in
to watch the retarded news,
and when the woman and I
broke up, when everything fell apart
and I loaded up my truck and drove off
into the broken world, they smiled
and waved from their porch, where they sat
every afternoon on the glider,
smiling and waving.

And now
Brahms is growing more anxious
and the little girl is calling
insanely in the distance
to the retarded little boy
who cannot answer, and this,
I recall, is the duet
my wife and I screamed
at each other through that long
final act, and I know that forevermore
all beautiful songs to me
will have their counterpoint of insanity,
that reminder that the world out there
is damaged beyond recovery.
So for God's sake
close the windows. Shut the door.

Turn up the music.

GOOD HUMOR

You don't often hear them anymore
but now and then a survivor
of The Great Ice Cream Truck Purges
at the end of the last century

approaches with its sad little tune
from a far street, on the last page
of the Book of Summer,

and even now this urge arises,
this panic to run inside
the house that is still there

to find the mother who is still sitting
at her Singer sewing machine
making a cotton shift for my sister
who is still in second grade,

and ask her, beg her, for the nickel
that will still buy the popsicle,
or drumstick, or orange fifty-fifty bar
from the foggy cave of the truck

whose music may be drawing closer now,
or moving farther away;
at this distance it's hard to say.

HAYWIRE

When I was a kid,
there was always someone old
living with my friends,
a small, gray person
from another century
who stayed in a back room
with a Bible and a bed with silver rails.

They were from a time before the time
the world just plain went haywire,

and even though nothing
made sense to them anymore,
they'd gotten used to it,
and walked around smiling vaguely
at the aliens ruining the galaxy
on the color console television,

or the British invasion
growing from the sides of our heads
in little transistorized boxes.

In the front room, by the light of tv,
we were just starting to get stoned,
and the girls were helping us
help them out of their jeans,

while in the back room
someone very tired
closed her eyes and watched
a wheat field where a boy
whose name she can't remember
is walking down a dusty road.

No sound
but the sound of crickets.
No satellites,
or even headlights in the distance yet.

CASABLANCA

Last night I saw *Casablanca* again,
following it like an old song
as it touched on all the familiar notes
of passion, betrayal, and death,

sweeping me along as helplessly
and willingly as it did the first time.

Once more I lamented
the lovers' lost idyll in Paris,
once more I sweated out with them
the approaching thunder of the Occupation,

and once more I felt the sweet relief
as the Nazis arrived at the airport
a split-second too late

to stop Bergman and Bogart
from climbing aboard the shining airplane
and rising toward freedom in a driving rain.

It's the same feeling I have every time
I come to the end of *Othello,*
when the Moor listens to Iago's
outrageous insinuations in utter disbelief
before having him whipped and imprisoned for life,

and then embarking with Desdemona
on a honeymoon cruise through the Aegean.

Or when, in the final, grainy frames,
the handsome young President in the open car
kisses Jackie with unabashed vigor,

and all the spectators on the grassy knoll
put down their cameras for a moment
and burst into spontaneous applause
as the limo returns triumphantly to the airport.

It's like that giddy feeling I had,
that sense of having steppped from a cave
into a bright meadow full of flowers,
when the doctors announced
that the looming gray mass on my mother's spine
had turned out to be nothing more
than a harmless flyspeck on the negative,

a feeling of pure, high-octane joy
of the sort I haven't experienced
since the day my wife came back to me in tears,

begging me to forgive her
for even considering the possibility
of leaving me. And of course I forgave her,

and held her for a long time
before taking her out to Mario's,
where we like to go on Friday night,

and the waiter brought us to our usual table
and the evening ended as evenings do

when there's been a little too much wine,
and the woman is very beautiful
and a sudden rain makes everything shine.

NORELCO

Adam had his father's face.
Telemachus had his father's bow.
And the sons of lost soldiers
have a German pistol
or a Japanese sword,
the sterner stuff
the old man was made of.

But all I have
from the last days of my dad
is his electric shaver,
egg-sleek, heavy
as a grenade,
with a thick black cord
and a gold *Norelco*
fading and nearly gone.

Sometimes I plug it in, click
the heavy switch to On.

As a younger man
he loved to watch me
watch him in the mirror:
straight razor,
brush and lather,
the four-foot leather strop.

But near the end, the DT's
made the lean blade dangerous.
I press the shaver to my cheek
and feel its cold mouth tremble
like his goodnight kiss.

WHAT WOULD JESUS DO?

—for dubya

Had Christ died, through sheer
Roman ingenuity, in the electric chair,

His hair would have lifted
in a spiky halo,
each filament pointing toward a sin.

His eyes would have widened
like the craziest prophet's, blazing
with the knowledge of a man or god
who has looked at lightning from the inside out.

From His mouth he would have spoken
smoke, and His tongue would have wagged
and stammered on the blue vowel
of a blowtorch, of Hell's pilot light,

while His fingernails curled and blackened like leaves,
His sacred testicles fulminated,

and from every orifice
rained the holy water
of the Son of God.

Thenceforth, penitents in all the churches
would shuffle forth every Sunday
to touch the True Electric Chair,

and weep over the Lord's Electrodes,
the heavy duty circuitry
that blew Him from the world,

while from silver necklaces
He would hang suspended in his Chair, enthroned

between the breasts of pretty girls
in shopping malls and movie theaters,

dying for us all and forever
as He did that day the voltage flowed

and the lights in the whole village
dimmed, then came back on, brighter than ever.

UNWISE PURCHASES

They sit around the house
not doing much of anything: the boxed set
of the complete works of Verdi, unopened.
The complete Proust, unread:

The French-cut silk shirts
which hang like expensive ghosts in the closet
and make me look exactly
like the kind of middle-aged man
who would wear a French-cut silk shirt:

The reflector telescope I thought would unlock
the mysteries of the heavens
but which I only used once or twice
to try to find something heavenly
in the windows of the high-rise down the road,
and which now stares disconsolately at the ceiling
when it could be examining the Crab Nebula:

The 30-day course in Spanish
whose text I never opened,
whose dozen cassette tapes remain unplayed,

save for Tape One, where I never learned
whether the suave American
conversing with a sultry-sounding desk clerk
at a Madrid hotel about the possibility
of obtaining a room,
actually managed to check in.

I like to think
that one thing led to another between them
and that by Tape Six or so
they're happily married
and raising a bilingual child in Seville or Terra Haute.

But I'll never know.

Suddenly I realize
I have constructed the perfect home
for a sexy, Spanish-speaking astronomer
who reads Proust while listening to Italian arias,

and I wonder if somewhere in this teeming city
there lives a woman with, say,
a fencing foil gathering dust in the corner
near her unused easel, a rainbow of oil paints
drying in their tubes

on the table where the violin
she bought on a whim
lies entombed in the permanent darkness
of its locked case
next to the abandoned chess set,

a woman who has always dreamed of becoming
the kind of woman the man I've always dreamed of becoming
has always dreamed of meeting.

And while the two of them discuss star clusters
and Cézanne, while they fence delicately
in Castilian Spanish to the strains of *Rigoletto,*

she and I will stand in the steamy kitchen,
fixing up a little risotto,
enjoying a modest cabernet,
while talking over a day so ordinary
as to seem miraculous.

VIEW OF THE CITY OF DELFT

In Vermeer's *View of the City of Delft*
the city beckons from a dreamy void—

but wait!   Hold on a minute.

Poems about paintings, poems you know
were written during some kind of travel grant
by a Guggenheim Fellow crazed with loneliness,

remind me of that moment on a first date
when you realize it's not going anywhere,

that the slim, delicious thoughts
you'd noticed slipping around the corners
of the workdays all week, like sylphs
idling in the palace chambers,

weren't looking at you after all.

They were waiting for someone
you'll never be, so you might as well
go back to the unspectacular
weather of the town you live in,
plain and steady as an old table,

where no fair creature of an hour,
smelling of musk and honeysuckle,
will draw you deliriously down
to the dark thunderhead of a nipple.

No. You two will be friends, and that's nothing
to sneeze at, friendship being precious and rare.

Count yourself lucky
that things between you will remain
as they are, safely in their frame,
like Vermeer's masterpiece,

in which the streets and buildings,
in all their stolid respectability,
are suspended forever

between an unattainable heaven
and the silent river, wherein
the city dreams, and darkens, and drowns.

ANNIVERSARY

I would like to keep lying here,
looking through the airy head of the elm tree, where clouds
go drifting through the blue gaps,

like the great white fish of summer,
swimming slowly through the ocean
of my day. Of my life.

And it would be nice to keep watching the tiny speck
of that high-circling, big-winged hawk
floating as easily in the sky
as I float on the summer grass.

But someone sitting on a bench
across the park is wearing a particular perfume,
and the breeze carries just a hint of it,
a couple of thousand molecules—

so now the simple act of breathing

reminds me of the way she used to touch her breasts
very lightly with that little glass wand
before our dinner parties,

and so for no reason
anyone watching me could guess,

I gather my books and newspaper, stand up
and stroll away, as if
I had some better place to be.

THE TABLE

I'm helping my brother-in-law
knock apart an old table
by the tool shed, a table they've loaded
with planting pots and fertilizer bags
for years, until a decade outside
in wind and rain has done it in.

And suddenly, as in a myth
or fairytale when the son
recognizes his lost father under the rags
of an old beggar, I realize
it's the kitchen table of our childhood,

where my mother and my two sisters and I
regathered and regrouped inside
a new house in a new state
after the divorce,

the dinner-time table
where we talked about our day,
practicing our first fictions
over pork chops and mashed potatoes
when Mom had a job, or fish sticks
or fried Spam, or chicken pot pies
when she didn't.

Where we dyed
our Easter eggs, and played through
rainy days of Scrabble.
Where I sweated over algebra
and the infernal verbs of the Germans,

and our mother would finish
a bottle of wine
and lay her head down and weep
over everything, terrifying us

into fits of good behavior,
of cleaning and vacuuming, until
she snapped out of it,
as if nothing had happened
and made it up to us
by doing something crazy
like making pancakes for supper.
The table where my uncle
got me drunk for the first time
and where I sat down to dinner
for the last time with my grandmother.

The table where my sister
announced she was pregnant,
where I said that, on the whole,
Canada had a lot more to offer
than Vietnam.
Where the four of us warmed ourselves
at the fire of family talk.

Plain brown table of ten thousand meals.

I'm starting to sweat now, the hammer
overmatched by iron-grained walnut
bolted at the joists. It takes a wrench
and a crowbar to finally break it down

to a splintered skeleton,
to the wreckage of an old table,
built when things were meant to last,

like a hardcover book, or a cathedral,
or a family. We stack up what's left
for firewood, and call it a day.

CHINESE

All the girls this summer are Chinese,
so sexy in their iPods, their Goon Squad
t-shirts, God, they drive me crazy!

They've got that look, that sleepy,
ancient, fog-shrouded hotness,
but they don't give a shit
about the Tang Dynasty or Zen,
No lacquered bowls for them.
Just turn up the Wu Tang
and make the Starbuck's sizzle.

Let the Chinese girls
play with their starry hair
spun of black holes and antimatter,
let them close the temples
of their eyes and dream
of silken algorithms, let the dumb
kids in the back of the class
look up in wonder at their smooth-assed
porcelain IQs, while the dazed
boys graze in the pastures
of their beauty, and the poor
American chicklets stand around,
stunned and deposed, saying
like, like, like—

Like you can do anything about it.
It's over, get used to it, you're
toast, you blond retard, the Chinese
are multiplying like bees
in the honeycombs of their cities,
their breasts are full of physics,
their eyes are dark
with quarks, their nipples
are destroying our libraries!

III

SHE'S GOOD

Right down to the very end, DiMaggio
insisted that whenever the horse-toothed,
doddering old ghost
the years had somehow made of him

was trundled out for yet another banquet
or home opener or old geezerfest,
they introduce him as
the world's greatest living ballplayer—

and the old geezers would clap
and get all misty-eyed
and the young women in little dresses
who knew him only as a line in some old song
or as that coffee guy,
just smiled and thought, as usual,
about their own beauty.

He was a fool, of course,
to hang around so long.
Marilyn could have told him
that the young favorites of the gods
are doomed, or should be, etc.

Despite this,
when Agassi misses the crosscourt backhand
because he was a step slow getting there,
I actually find myself saying

to the young woman whose hand rests in mine
like a tourist visiting the ruins of the Coliseum,
I would have had that—

and she
because she is the reason
for all crosscourt passes, all hat tricks and home runs,

does not laugh,

or even smile indulgently,
but draws a little closer
and says, *Easily*.

Touchdown.

           Knockout.

  Oh yeah.

Nothin' but net.

WAITING

When the guy in the hairpiece and the cheap suit
asks me if I want to see my mother
as she lies in a back room, waiting,

I remember her, for some reason,
in a white swimsuit, on a yellow towel

on the sand at Crystal Lake,
pregnant with my sister,
waiting for me to finish examining
the sleek fuselage of a minnow,

the first dead thing I had ever seen,
before we went back to the cottage for lunch.

I remember her waiting up for my father
to come home from God knows where
in a Yellow Cab at 2 AM,

and waiting for me in the school parking lot
in our rusted blue station wagon
when whatever it was I was practicing for ran late.

I remember her, shoulders thrown back,
waiting in the unemployment line,
waiting for me to call, waiting for the sweet release

in the second glass of wine
after a long day working at the convalescent hospital
where everyone was waiting to die.

And I remember her waiting for me
at the airport when I got back from Japan,
waiting for everything to be all right,

waiting for her biopsy results.
    Waiting.

But when the guy in his ridiculous hairpiece
asks me if I'd like to go back there
and be with her in that room where she lies

waiting to be cremated, I say *No*
thank you, and turn and walk out
onto the sunny street to join the crowd

hustling down the sidewalk,
and I look up at the beautiful white clouds
suspended above the city,

leaving her to wait in that room alone,
for which I will not be forgiven.

MUSEUM PIECE
—for Carmi

Standing in front of this pint-sized fighter
   in his greaves and chain mail,
his jacket of chased steel,

   I think of my six-foot uncle
in the bomber
   he wore like a suit of armor.

He wore his B-52
   like a second skin.
Like he wore his white Cadillac

   and ten-gallon Stetson,
his wife and his Texas spread.
   Like he wore the war.

Mythic quester, little knight,
   your lance is much too small.
You'd never see him coming.

My uncle was a twinkle of light
   in his Stratofortress
and his enemies turned to dust.

And though he ended Vietnam
   with a Colt Python
in his paneled den,

for me he never came down.

In the shadow of his flight
   over the boiling land
there's nothing to destroy.

What's left for me
   but to build
the small museum
   of this poem for him?

OLYMPICS

One of the pixies on the U.S. team,
a little starveling kept from food
and boys and pretty much everything
in order to spend her teens
fending off puberty
from the cloister
of a balance beam,

gives a tiny wobble
when she touches down
after agitating the air above the mat
spectacularly—

So tiny, in fact,
that only the Russian judge
with the horse trader's eye
can even see it. But just like that
she's lost a thousandth of a point,
the gold, the silver, even the bronze.

And she stands there sobbing
in the arms of her coach,
an actual woman
with a monthly period
and the luxury of breasts,

who looks at her little failure
with an expression I remember
on the face of my ex-wife

when I wobbled on the balance beam
of our marriage, missed the vault
into bed, came home late
from the uneven bars.

DARK SIDE OF THE MOON

I walk down to the bay,
an after-dinner stroll in the darkness.
and there, on the invisible horizon,
is the red, lacquered bowl
of the quarter moon, just beginning
to sink into the Pacific,
not far from where I watched
the sun go down
only a few hours earlier.

So in one day I've seen
the sun set and the moon set.
And though nothing is more predictable
than when and where the sun will vanish,
I couldn't tell you anything
about the habits of the moon.

Some nights you see it up there—a ball
or a bowl or a thin white smile—
and some nights you don't.

It's a mystery
I want to talk to you about
after I walk back home
and climb into bed,
where I know you will be deep
in a novel as usual,
one side of your face
lit by the yellow reading lamp,
one side in shadow.

GOING TO BED

I check the locks on the front door
        and the side door,
make sure the windows are closed
        and the heat dialed down.
I switch off the computer,
        turn off the living room lights.

I let in the cats.

        Reverently, I unplug the Christmas tree,
leaving Christ and the little animals
        in the dark.

The last thing I do
        is step out to the back yard
for a quick look at the Milky Way.

        The stars are halogen-blue.
The constellations, whose names
        I have long since forgotten,
look down anonymously,
        and the whole galaxy
is cartwheeling in silence through the night.

        Everything seems to be ok.

CITIZEN KANE

All summer and fall
my Flexible Flyer
clung like a moth
to the basement wall.

Then would come that morning
when white was the only color,
when the school bus couldn't come,
and my father took it down.

He waxed the red runners
and we went outside together.
The world was ours to explore.

When I die, I can't imagine
the last thing I'll remember,
the last words I will say.

But I want death
to be like my father
in his big boots and heavy sweater,
lifting down my sled for winter,
taking me with him into the day.

GLOBAL WARMING

A bunch of kids, flies in their eyes,
    are starving on the new flat-screen
        as we sit in the bar, far from Africa.
There's a number you can call,
        but no one writes it down.

One hundred degrees today. A record.
    The beer is very cold.
        And that's
the current situation in Cleveland.

 Except there's another problem
with the space shuttle, some more of that foam
        has banged into the heat tiles
Which no one, absolutely no one,
        can figure out how to glue on so they'll stay.

It's starting to look like we'll never make it
    off this planet,
                all because of some lousy glue.

    But nonetheless,
the astronauts are smiling, cheerful and upside down,
        although the token Asian guy
looks a little worried, a bit apprehensive
    about reentry.
                Even Tokyo in the summer—
trains packed with sweaty salarymen, earthquakes
        every five minutes—
                has to be looking pretty good right now.

        But I, for one,
am safe. Safe and well-informed. Magma
        cooled. Velociraptors
    turned to gasoline.
        Life became a magazine.

All of which occurred
        just to bring me here
    to this stool. This apogee.

I have stood on the shoulders of giants.

I am where the astronauts and the starving kids
        would like to be,
                                cool and a little buzzed,
        full of common sense.
Faithfully serving my role as audience.

        I could sit here forever…

But tonight Jodie's making gazpacho,
    and she has a heavy hand with the cilantro.

And Gary is bringing the chardonnay
        he got this summer in Napa,
    and Roger has fresh blueberries for dessert.

So now I must pop the heavy hatchway
        leading from my pressurized capsule
into a heat that is breaking records

in a dying city at the end of the world
        where, despite everything,
    we're all reasonably happy.

ABOUT THE AUTHOR

George Bilgere is the author is three previous collections of poetry, *The Going* (University of Missouri Press), *Big Bang* (Copper Beech), and *The Good Kiss* (University of Akron Press). His poems have appeared in such periodicals and anthologies as *Poetry, The Sewanee Review, Ploughshares, The Southern Review,* and *Best American Poetry.* A recipient of grants from the National Endowment for the Arts, The Fulbright Commission, the Witter Bynner Foundation, and the Ohio Arts Council, he is a professor of English at John Carroll University.

Bilgere received the 2006 Ohioana Poetry Award, a prize given yearly to an Ohio poet for a body of published work that has made, and continues to make, a significant contribution to poetry, and through whose work as a writer, teacher, administrator, or in community service, interest in poetry has been developed.

THE MAY SWENSON
POETRY AWARD

This annual competition, named for May Swenson, honors her as one
of America's most provocative and vital poets. In the words of John
Hollander, she was "one of our few unquestionably major poets."
During her long career, May was loved and praised by writers from
virtually every major school of poetry. She left a legacy of nearly fifty
years of writing when she died in 1989.

May Swenson lived most of her adult life in New York City, the
center of American poetry writing and publishing in her day. But she
is buried in Logan, Utah, her birthplace and hometown.